Shoogle

GW00722559

Earlyworks Press Poetry

Shoogle Tide

Earlyworks Press Poetry

'For the Long Down Road' by Clive Gilson first published in 'Writing on Water' Ragged Raven 2005 ISBN 09542397-8-4

ISBN 978-0-9553429-7-4

Published by Earlyworks Press
Creative Media Centre
45 Robertson St, Hastings
Sussex TN34 1HL

www.earlyworkspress.co.uk

Contents

Title	Author	Page
Hanging over Rio	Margaret Eddershaw	1
Coffee Break	Poul Webb	2
St. Peter's By Night	Sylvia Oldroyd	3
Cantata For Voices and Cafeteria	Anne Ayres	4
Insides (Hanoi on my Bike)	Marianne Brown	5
Pink	Marianne Brown	6
The Rain Cycle	Ruary O Siochain	7
Changes	Catherine Edmunds	8
Riot Weather	R D Gardner	9
City	Poul Webb	10
The Rite of Spring	R D Gardner	11
A Sense of History	David R Morgan	12
Secret Windings	Victoria Seymour	13
For the Long Down Road	Clive Gilson	14
Arif's Legs	Clive Gilson	15
Watching the News	Jenny Hamlett	16
A Midden	Nick McCarty	17
Smaller Magic	David R Morgan	18
Journey Without End	Phil Powley	19
Come As You Are	Jo Else	
Calum	Jo Else	20
The Gravity of Yearning	Ruary O Siochain	21
Moonstruck	Phil Powley	22
In Transit	Sylvia Oldroyd	23
The Museum Ship's Manifest	Anne Ayres	24
Luck	Nigel Humphreys	25
Killing Time	Marilyn Francis	26
The Boy on the Camden Omnibus	Catherine Edmunds	27
The Vagrant	Alison Craig	28
Creatures in the Sky	Gilly Jones	29
Standing Stone	Steve Mann	30
Green Fly High	Catherine Edmunds	31
Drowned	Catherine Edmunds	32
Return to Haworth	Jenny Hamlett	33

Bardy	David R Morgan	34
In Loving Memory of Lily Yeates	Marilyn Francis	35
Funeral In Rome	Sylvia Oldroyd	36
Missing Cousins	Nigel Humphreys	37
What is Home?	Michael Heery	38
Family Holiday	Amy Licence	39
Ancient Woodland	Michael Heery	41
Lament: Britain BC	David Dennis	42
Where Waters Meet	John Appleyard	43
Horse Standing Motionless	Duncan Fraser	44
A Visual Feast	Angela Bradley	45
The Wasp	Keith Shaw	46
Joni in Big Yellow Marigolds	R D Gardner	47
Each Fall I Rise	Valentin Barrios-Ambroa	48
Reading the Diaries	Andria J Cooke	49
Falling in Love with Emma Peel	Clive Gilson	50
Stray Cat	Stephen Firth	51
Play it Again, Sam	Andria J Cooke	52
Days When Women Dance	r v jones	53
Landlines	Andria J Cooke	54
The Exchange of Chocolate for a Secret	Gilly Jones	55
Pearl	Margaret Eddershaw	56
Peter Likes to Laugh	Marilyn Francis	57
Brief Sparkling Moments	Gilly Jones	58
Empty Nest Syndrome	R J Hansford	59
Heave, Rewind	r v jones	60
Chemotherapy	Michael Heery	61
Nil By Mouth	Valentin Barrios-Ambroa	62
A Special Way of Being Afraid	r v jones	63
Where Does Truth Come From?	Amy Licence	64
Vermicelli	Nigel Humphreys	65
The Komodo Dragon	Karl Ghattas	66
Poetry Is…	Phil Powley	67
Fertility	R J Hansford	67
Secret Windings	Marilyn Francis	68

Hanging Over Rio

Run
run down a jutting platform
at five thousand feet
eyes on the horizon
bold as a fledgling leaving its nest
run into space
till weightless.

Thermal over
Rio's rainforest lungs
that heave and bunch like
green coral in limpid water
crowding colonial facades
legoland skyscrapers
hotels with roof-gardens and winking pools.

Arms outstretched
soar like Christ the Redeemer
who gazes at another shrine
the Maracana Football Stadium
while at his feet
a scramble of favelas
is poised to mudslide
onto their unequal neighbours.

Glide out to embrace the misty bay
turn for a homing pigeon's view
of the city patchwork
framed by peaks
fringed with a fly-paper strip
between tarmac and ocean.

Sigh down, down
soft as a feather in a draught
to make footprints
in caster sugar sand.

Margaret Eddershaw

Coffee Break

On polished tables
buns dusted with icing
languor in serrated cups.
Fractured sunlight glints
on faux Bauhaus chairs –
neon slabs creeping across
a pockmarked cubist floor.
Tree shadows speckled
on red slatted benches
where giro collectors gather
with their brindled dogs.
A girl of sixteen sits
on her boyfriend's lap –
a pink dummy in her mouth –
hooped earrings big enough
for the dogs to jump through,
and two black eyes
that turn out to be mascara.
The sun is very low –
glows on the green copper
domes of the opera house
that has never echoed
to the bellow of a baritone,
and where opera glasses
now come in halves and pints.
Wet paviors in the square
are shining like glass –
innuit on sleds glide past,
and a man playing
doleful dirges on a crumpled
trumpet stands beneath
the millennium clock
that stopped
in nineteen ninety-nine.

Poul Webb

St. Peter's By Night

Known constellations
cast their mesh
over an unfamiliar skyline;

above the Vatican,
Ursa Major dangles
the bait of its tail-end star.

Bernini's pillared colonnades
draw imperceptibly tighter;
Seine net in stone.

The dome, wrapped in light
the colour of a halo,
shelters the fisherman's tomb;

shoulders the universe.

Sylvia Oldroyd

Cantata For Voices and Cafeteria

The opening chords are high-pitched, young,
undisciplined. They are answered by soothing
lower tones. High, low, high, low, chair scrapes,
cutlery clatters, cash register rings, money falls.

The sopranos and tenors flow in like a river
around the tables and chairs. The highest notes
soar to reach the very corners of the ceiling. The
baritones vibrate the air. The cash register rings.

The words are indistinct. The babble, gabble,
jabber, gibber surges and retreats. The central
melody becomes discordant, random phrases
are detached. A chair scrapes and money falls.

The finale fast approaches with repetitions of
earlier refrains and a rush of steam; a fallen
chair; a crying child; a burst of laughter and for
one fleeting moment a crescendo of pure silence.

Anne Ayres

Insides
(Hanoi on my bike)

Chewed up
from the dust as trucks hurtle past
beep rashes, close shaves
rattled loose brakes

Sucked
into an unlit lane, arched orifice lined with lumpy doorways
emptying glass displays; eggs milk bread entrails,
scraping stray children 'heh-lo' 'whatsoname'
gritty veins pump everything out
through the incense pork skin sewage haze
 - but there's something cool and leafy
in the heart - I'm squeezed into it

lake

road ends drink the quiet

water sips the sky

Marianne Brown

Pink

Shocked me

as I pushed through 5am on the dyke road.

Houses seeped into the tarmac,
pores clogged with city sweat,
I thought I was saturated

And then: jelly pink wobbled by
             on the back of a motorbike
             mouths jiggled open
             holes poked in the froth

No sudden gaping red
No scarlet gash

Only sweet fat pink
sugar pink
ripe open
pink

Marianne Brown

The Rain Cycle

Cycling through the city streets in rain
the thought marks, blots and seeps
edge further the spoken spray
damp awareness setting hold
of soggy nethers, a wet forest.

In the old days
stand astride a blazing fire
In the old days
clap a cabman on the back
In the old days
sink a single malt for comfort
In the old days
catch your death the servants way.

I'm enjoying this wetly bath
my two legs motor launch the bicycle,
ethereal the clam cold hold
of trouser fabric, but my shoes
become two paddles too.

These days
there's no excuse for wetness
These days
high tech fabric wicks damp away
These days
the venting systems on my car perform
These days
ignore the laws on climate change.

Two wheels rotavate the puddles
a wash suspending waves of thought
dissolve the weary car soaked traffic
and there allow the moment happen:
I'm singing, I'm singing, Hap hap hap....

Ruary O Siochain

7

Changes

a starling hurls itself at my window
survives
leaves angry
it won't be back until it forgets

next door's hammering yet again
breaking bricks
where once he built, now he destroys
next he will build again

too many cycles

time to move on to a house with small windows
that no bird would ever mistake for the sky
time to eat lettuce grow parsley wild strawberries
find rhythms and counterpoint layers of meaning
draw horses paint artichokes eat lemon pie

easy to do
the slightest thought may produce the butterfly
I've spied a banana next to a paintbrush
I have an idea
watch out, watch out for hurricanes

Catherine Edmunds

Riot Weather

There are worse things than clouds, weathergirl –
there is the office with welded windows
where the fan turns slowly, slowly,
winding up the heat and letting it fall
and cooling nothing at all.

There are worse things than rain, weathergirl –
there is the weary back and forth of the watering can
to the stunted beans, and lettuces translucent
and flat as seaweed when the tide's long out,
while the dead lawn crunches underfoot.

There are worse things than gales, weathergirl –
there is a sleepless bed in a locked-down bedroom,
the fevered light of sodium gnawing the blinds
and the leaden dread of half-dream trapped in the sheet
that winds itself around your clammy heat.

There is you, our pretty blonde weathergirl –
your white hands dancing on your magic map
as you promise us 'yet another beautiful day,
though parts of Scotland just might see some rain:
won't that be a shame?'

There are worse things than storms, weathergirl.
Do you hear the tap-tap-tapping at your window pane?
It isn't rain.

R D Gardner

City

Strobing through naked branches, orange filtered sunlight
shadow-flickers on grimy windows, sparks on the curves
of cars creeping across the waking city.
Double-decker faces peer from steamed-up buses
that diesel-rumble along slippy shiny roads.
iPodded pedestrians, briefcased
and laptopped plod towards their towers
of concrete, steel and glass where money
gently hums to a pinstriped rhythm.
Beneath café awnings aluminium
chairs are being unstacked,
sandwich boards unfolded.
Inside, the jarring sound of coffee
being ground, the hiss and whistle
of an espresso machine.
The first customers ordering
lattes and cappuccinos –
takeaways in cardboard cups.
People carrying things –
window cleaners with squeegees,
postmen with heavy sacks,
groceries from the metro-store,
designer shopping bags,
bottles of designer water,
umbrellas, and a guitar case.
Biffa bins being lifted,
emptied into sturdy trucks –
the heave and slide of life's
detritus consigned
to the landfill
of history.

Poul Webb

The Rite of Spring

Nobody pipes for the girls at the crossroads.
The man with the bodhrán is timing his pint
And the fiddler is raising his elbow.

Nobody plays for the maidens of May,
The crop-topped and hair-jewelled girl queens of today.

Untiring musicians called up at the crossroads:
A little black boom-box sits snug by the wall
And its drum-machines skitter and prattle.

Pump up the volume, twirl, throw up your hands –
Last year's Top Forty, bleached Girl Power bands.

One tall as a birch tree, jewelled hearts on her T-shirt,
One small as a bottle of ribboned champagne.
Out of step, out of time, wannabe Eurovision,
Where the town's four roads meet, in the morning, in May.

Nobody pipes in the dark at the crossroads,
Where low roads run out into County Roscommon,
A waning moon rising beyond them.

Grandmother, Grandmother, let down your grey hair.
The girls' little boom-box squats close as a toad
At the finger-post's base, and old ladies in black
Are dancing death metal, at night, in the road.

R D Gardner

A Sense of History

They say,
It is quite something to lose.
It is quite something to be wrong;
To give one's precious life to the passing gale;
To forsake all but the distant hosannas of the unseen stars
And still then to be one's own.

They say,
Such a being may stand on the high hill called Hero
And shadow the bland blue sky
With the back of his rightness-steady hand
And for him,
As for the headline glory of a terrible victory,
Ten million men shall die.

They say this
And smile, satisfied, as some worm presses the final button alone;
And no mouths are left to speak of legends,
No hand to write the great book of records...
And all the jolly journalists catch fire before they use their phones.

David R Morgan

Secret Windings

Twisting through eroded brick, petrified timbers and sand rock
narrow alleys, once the way of smugglers or fishermen,
steady sea-legs landlubbered by drink that robbed the table.
Barefoot children ran among the windings
to escape a father's blow or truncheon justice.
Ragged fishwives whispered across thresholds
the advent of another mouth to cry hunger.

The post-war visionaries cleared the slums,
tore out the entrails of an organism seven centuries old.
Vestiges give passage to artists, poets
chic newcomers and drunkards,
who grease the ancient footpaths with piss and vomit.

Victoria Seymour

13

For The Long Down Road

It comes like hallelujah, an evangelical chorus,
a beating of breasts in the red light of deep nights,
a commitment, the full bore, whole-hog embrace,
a snaking line of party hats and staccato elbows,
the speaking in tongues that comes by degree
rather than absolute shocking blue revelation.

It is the host, the revel, arms locked in arms,
the break of dance and palsied eye, the sleepless lids
and sallow skin that bids farewell poor innocence,
a learning of rules and words in cups, draughted
and drawn, the drinking down of the long road
that winds its easy path along the ways of lost days.

This is a serious dedication to alcohol in low light places,
chosen because your smile can't be seen among so many
lunatic grins, where you become faceless among the beloved,
and so, in the company of those who gutter in the wind
like you do, you slowly wind on the clock, tripping dully
through the sag of years until you run out of geography.

Clive Gilson

Arif's Legs

Flip-flops smack hard baked sand,
a rhythmic chattering beneath the soft glide
of cheap silk sarongs and ludicrously loud
beach shirts. Cracked earth and spare weeds
line a path that passes bare tables
in the yawning shadows of a Nepalese restaurant.
Arif swings out of the shade and waits
in the sun on a corner. He squats, smiling,
in the company of mangy mongrels,
lounging the day away, waiting,
for half finished meals and overflowing bins at dusk.
In the down draught of beer guts and sweat
Arif's limbs jut and break at right angles.
He crawls on one bent leg, propelled
forwards by one smashed and twisted arm.
His left hand bends impossibly backwards.
His right arm, his good arm is raised,
palm upwards and creased with dirt.
Flint brown eyes glint as he smiles
under the spindle bower, with dogs
scratching their arses and the sores
behind their ears. Arif waits, counting
the slap of fat footfalls, preparing his smile.
Seeing colours emerge from the heat haze,
Arif shuffles out onto the path, beams,
and knowing the many colours of money,
declares his eternal love for Manchester United.

Clive Gilson

15

Watching the News

Since I cannot put the world to rights, I speak of love
John Gower

Each evening from armchair-comfort
the news drags us into a thicket of brambles.
We are snagged on the last train crash,
rip our fingers in the latest political mess
and bleed each time terrorists set off
another bomb in Iraq until we long for nothing
except the blind, hypnotic, rhythm
of the shipping forecast.

Then one morning a newspaper prints
the photograph of a man on a broken box
in front of a half-destroyed home,
amongst debris from the aftermath
of a Baghdad car bomb. He is reading
his poetry to the few who dare the streets,
the language, in this barren city of dust,
is a fountain of chipped love.

Jenny Hamlett

A Midden

Who came here before us
Heard seas hissing over rolling pebbles
At the edge.

Who came here before us
Watched red shanks skittering over
Black musseled rocks.

Who came here before us
Listened to the mewing pale plovers
In a winter morning
And the calls of other men
Across the sand and scything marram
At the edge.

Piled high and buried deep
Propping the dunes guarding
The Bay of Golden Plovers
A cairn built of crumbling shards
Of molluscs lies in layers at the edge.
A graveyard monument of clams and oysters
To those who came before and saw
The sea mists roll over the dunes
Sat and shivered in damp cold
A mystery to the watchers at the edge.

Those before fed on orange mussels
Used the shells for scraper, cup and blade
Then left behind a memorial
To those who heard the broken call of plovers
Standing in the eddying water at the edge.

A midden left by those who stood and stared
Across silky water at a lifting sun
To see the light sharp over a rim of stone
At the edge

                          Nick McCarty

17

Smaller Magic

My home lay in the heart
of the angled forest,
far from rhyming pasture.

Honeysuckle swam like a fiery sea,
stags dipped their horned heads in welcome
and stayed still for me and silent.

Light as floss I soared through green heaven,
fast as dappled light
and in the oak cool dark birds fanned my hair.

Now I trace the smaller magic
on your city's edges,
counting axe strokes through clouded years.

David R Morgan

Journey Without End

Sometimes I have an urge to jump a train
that's pulling out, be ferried far away
to fabled Camelot or Dunsinane,
intending just to travel, not to stay.
And I'd expect this odyssey to heal
my troubled mind, allow me to break free
from worry's chains that clank and squeal.
Of course, it wouldn't work like that. I'd see
grey skies, tired homes, industrial estates
and sodden fields. But then the clouds might part,
a shaft of sunshine gild a steeple's slates;
a traveller's smile might lighten my dull heart.
And as we slowed, long after we were due,
the boy I was would wave as we passed through.

Phil Powley

Come As You Are

Drop your sword to the ground
empty your revolver on the floor
remove the visor covering your face,
loosen the shirt with the hundred buttons,
and let me see you
unshed, uncorrupted
pure in the moonlight,
as you were at 18
pale jewel at my throat
before they scarred you,
with life.

Jo Else

Calum

open calm moon, your face
cream curtains, kitchen, blue check,
spring to mind come wholesome things, freeing me.
bread and wine, from brown grained tables
dispense communion,
expand our afternoon with shore light,
walks and shells,
specks of my attainable unhappiness are gone for good;
in beaches bright with lanterns
we crackle by spring fires, speaking.

Jo Else

The Gravity of Yearning

There is a film
taken from Space, it
shows the oceans bulge
and in tidal swell
pull towards the arid moon
in plastic yearning,
a pure desire that sleeps
when the moon is cast
away on the other side.

With not enough left
for a single tear,
the Sea of Tranquillity
keens her loss,
like a sheep
to her lamb
penned in the web
of earthly gravity.

Ruary O Siochain

Moonstruck

It's a cold, clear night; you are going to watch
an eclipse of the moon.

Already you have set the oven timer alarm
to go off at 10 minute intervals.

You keep going in and out, leaving the
back door open. It's getting colder indoors.
I start to calculate what it will cost in oil
to get the temperature back up. 1500 litres
have just cost me £485.

The timer rings. You rush out: "It's started!"

I am sunk in the sofa with a glass of Guinness.

"Come and see."

I crawl out. A bit of moon is missing at the bottom.
I go back in and stay there. You rush in and out
ten times, digitally photographing each phase,
failing to shut the door.

Next morning we watch the 'sequence' on the VDU.
Ten moons (of different sizes!) turning from white
to black. A small red stain on one apparently indicates
the success of your mission.

"What do you think?"

"Very nice."

"Is that all?"

It's true. You and I live on different planets.

Phil Powley

In Transit

Crossing the disc
the pea-sized silhouette
looks like the stem-scar
on a slow-rotating orange.

Mindful of ultra-violet,
I watch it safely on TV,
having to endure
the patter of presenters

urging me to note
the exact time of Third Contact
and send it by email
in order to get my very own

calculation of the sun's distance
from earth; a measurement
known since 1769.
Cameras flick from Greenwich

to Much Hoole, the place
of first recorded transit.
I want only to contemplate
the six-hour trace of a curve,

to salute this sun-child seen
by day for the first and final time;
Venus, dark morning-star,
Sister-ship sailing our deep of space.

Sylvia Oldroyd

The Museum Ship's Manifest

This is a true list of our cargo -

Saxon warriors of warlike disposition
and their downtrodden wives who are
tasked with all domestic duties while
their menfolk conquer new territories.

Roman citizens whose administrative
skills have a proven track record; also
their highly trained craftsmen and captive
slaves; male and female; willing or not.

Medieval merchants whose bargaining
skills will doubtless serve us well and
machiavellian courtiers who are able to
negotiate treaties on favourable terms.

Here are railway engineers; boat builders;
ale brewers; scribes, clerics and artisans.
Also on board are numerous visitors whose
expertise may become apparent in transit.

All is shipshape; the cargo secured; hatches
battened; the vessel ready to weigh anchor.
The course is plotted and like Columbus we
will bravely sail away to an uncertain future.

Anne Ayres

Luck

is the very devil when he bastes;
he has glow and spin, a venereal voice extruding
lures like forced rhubarb,
touts a sneak look at the answers

he took me to the top floor
once
made me look down on the gambling tables:
white balls pimping red and black, court cards
coming on from the baize

his arm eeled around my shoulders and he made me
listen to the clash of coin
dazzled me with cartoon arithmetic and tumbling fruit
offered me kinds of foreknowledge.
an express way out
the fleeting membership of a club where long odds
lap dance for my favours

I was tempted
scooped the dice, cooled their snake eyes

but those same odds could give me cancer, strike me
with lightning and in that thought's heat
his visor melted and I knew him
for a sleight of mind, an exceptional resolution
where probability would have been the very devil.

Nigel Humphreys

Killing Time

Marooned in the endless summer
afternoon of my seventh year
scuffing the red Clark's sandals idly
at the curb-stone
willing something
to happen
I checked my tick-tock Timex watch -
time had stopped.
Dead.

Yesterday I checked the deathclock
it said I will die in my
seventy seventh year
to heaven
I had only 642,686,343
seconds left
to kill.

Maybe I'll make a model
of the Eiffel Tower
in Swan Vestas.

Marilyn Francis

The Boy on the Camden Omnibus

a tiny goth stayed over last night
so petite, you could put her in your pocket
she said thank you very nicely and left to get her bus

I'm not sure who she was and will probably
never see her again.
he told me her name but I thought that was somebody else

it was

so he rolled his eyes and told me he never
would remove anything from my hi-fi
but on closer questioning it turns out that
perhaps he did

I've put it back
no harm done
I don't know what it is

he says it's the stereo one
not realising that 78s are mono
so it doesn't matter how I put them onto my pc

he walked the tiny goth down to the bus
she was probably bound for shildon or coundon
while he was going all the way to camden town

I must must must go down there soon

Catherine Edmunds

The Vagrant

High,
on a whim or a preset,
a breakaway tips its wings
triggers velocity
and feathers north,
where the sun lies undercover
like some shock creation of a white-coated science,
or a sailor's rope trick
reversing polarity
and switching summer playgrounds
to a higher latitude,
where a snowy silence
purses its lips
shutting light in like a secret.

Overhead,
a trailing edge brushes the clouds,
steers away from the ancestral tracks
those deep grooves that set course
for the mudholes and deltas,
where kind and alike
gather over rising thermals,
drinking spring melts,
and preening till twilight comes
when the forktailed foreman
with a quick flash of covert
delivers them to the wind
swirling and circling
over the sandbanks,
to forage in oilspill
and scramble once again
at the bark of a dog.

Alison Craig

Creatures in the Sky

One cloud hangs in the sky,
bloated whale,
blotting out the sun,
mouth shape wide agape,
malevolent monster
that will swallow all the world,
or spew out more than Jonah ever saw,
waiting with winking watching eye,
spitefully surveying the scene below,
sullenly spreading,
stretching until
the sky is sagging
like a dirty wet sheet,
dripping spots of rain,
splashing drops down,
drenching everything until
the deluge stops,
releasing buoyant beasts
tumbling in the wide blue sky,
tangling and untangling
misty tendrils of dragons
breath in the air,
stretching like a silken skein
or a rope made of smoke,
creating new creatures
in the sky.

Gilly Jones

Standing Stone

standing tall grey apparent
firm place portal latch
hidden clear mystery held
otherworld knowing spirit catch

ancient heart life's sorrow
Male Female Sidhe
present be present they
otherworld knowing spirit see

wisdom's face once many
deep eyes looking deep
brow furrowed thoughts profound
otherworld knowing spirit keep

Steve Mann

Green Fly High

they left us in the garden for an hour or two
so what did they expect? maybe that was the plan

under the apple tree nothing would happen
unless
unless I did something drastic
so I put my arms around your shoulders
and pulled you to the ground
closed my eyes
because you are ugly, you know
quite hideous

eyes shut, you don't look so bad
and you know what to do with your hands
so the hour or two passed most pleasantly

then they came back
they'd been to the shops
and showed us their purchases
we smiled and nodded and said the right things

I left
but still
I remember your warm shoulders
as I pulled you down on the lawn
and your green fingers wove through my hair
awakening the soil beneath my body
the smell of crushed grasses, stinging ants, earthy breath
in my nostrils, bindweed capturing, tying me down and your arms
writhing tree roots, such strength, I never knew, never realised

recognition comes as the season of fire approaches
so that's who you were
I should have known
but you hid yourself well
beneath the old apple tree deep in the flowering grasses

Catherine Edmunds

Drowned

it's cold in this wind, I can't stand, need support,
I'm frightened of waves, of white horses, grey water.
the fellside is hidden in rain speckled shadow
(I was never so wet as in clouds).

once, long ago, I fought with the storm
but the wind blew my mind far away past the ghostly
white remnants of snow, still clinging where once
I wandered past hawthorns, but now only broken
brown bracken. the farm's gone away, long forgot.

today peewits fly, water's lap lapping, gentle
the ghosts sleep peacefully under green stones
past sun's noontime haze, long gone after drowning.
the heathery fells hold no threat, but remember
when storms couldn't harm me round lanes, fields and hedges
we sang and the laughter lasted forever
but drowning snuffs dawn out and presses my eyes shut
as brackish brown water lap laps life away

the wind and the rain whisper (still here) through clouds
still drowning unwary and wild the unknowing
the tempest still raging, the anger still crushing
the wilderness grasping the memories of loss
cold waters that frighten the song far away.

hush now; remember the storm clouds, the windsong,
the raining, the loss and the horses that ran
through the heather, remember the ringing beneath
the white water, remember we drowned long ago.

Catherine Edmunds

Return to Haworth

Cold in the earth – and the deep snow piled above thee...
- Emily Bronte

The pilgrim, drawn back and holding
the apparition of those low dark moors
climbs slowly on the paved way
leaving the valley and its clacking mills.
She finds black graves, a house alone on the hill

where Patrick shoots his church each morning
and his son lies drunk from a night
in The Black Bull. The girls work.
Charlotte sweeps floors, black-leads the stove.
Anne leans to mend a tower of clothes

and Emily reigns, queen in a muddle of crockery
as she kneads bread. She looks up,
Why do you come? *We don't need you.*
The pilgrim tries to answer but her mind is sealed.
Emily fetches her hound. *Chase her off,* she says.

So leaving the sisters to their imaginative lives,
to Emily's pretence their fame is myth,
the pilgrim trudges the grit-stone heath
where a cruel wind whips the bell heather
as their stories and poems whirl in her head.

Jenny Hamlett

Bardy

Windless sweat of a hot summer's day:
Bardy, inseparable from her bed,
each minute enormous,
watches dancing figures
flitting through the lacework of net curtains ...

ballerinas of light on illuminated floors of air
becoming to Bardy solid, living, moving,
until the whole room is inhabited by creatures of light;
a beauty no human words can compass or disclose.
She, pale as white roses, is static and dying ...

yet now her heart uplifts;
dead roses become berries to redden winter
to feed the coming spring.
Oh the bright creatures are glorious, *do not breathe*;
the quieter she becomes the more she can see ...

Until she is in total harmony living in hermetic light;
with it, as shadows come, she somersaults away
and when her family arrive,
through the thin dark door of reality,
Bardy is no longer there ...

David R Morgan

In Loving Memory of Lily Yeates (School Mistress)

Cold sunlight
cruel as a stiletto
bitter as a supermarket lemon
slices through shadow
makes all things clear.

Trudging, foot-clogged
through the tiers of the dead
to the sanctuary
of a weathered look-out
halfway to heaven
in this chill, still churchyard.

Beneath the bench marked
  In Affectionate Memory
  of Barbara Smoker RIP
the fag-ends of the bereaved lie
stubbed out forever. All around
the ranks of the dead bask
like Costa Brava bathers
in the sour sunlight.

A sudden sly crow-voiced breeze
carries shrill memories of
long-ago children at play
in the silent nettled schoolyard
far below.

Marilyn Francis

Funeral In Rome

He died in the octave of Easter
went straight to Heaven
on the back of the risen Christ
according to Polish myth

islanded in the Piazza
the plain cypress coffin
carries wounds of the living tree
mitred joints fashioned
in a carpenter's workshop

an April wind billows
cardinals' robes into turmoil of flame
flurries the coffin-lid Gospel's pages
closes its crimson cover
some say it was God's breath

Bernini's colonnades curve
to embrace the faithful
cupped hands receiving the wafer
a chalice of pillared stone

incense swirls among
black and gold of vestments
mingles with Latin litany
with prayer in a mix of tongues
cadences that need no translation

applause halts the ceremony
and chanting: *Giovanni Paolo!*
Giovanni Paolo! Santo subito!

the great bell of St. Peter's
welcomes him in

Sylvia Oldroyd

Missing Cousins

After the committal
in the bounce of relief on the sodden grass
a crows' murder in the skeletal trees
and the oboe low of anguish held fading

we,
each other's diminishing assets,
shake hands, speak through layers of sugar coating
and count our coinage in children's names

meet
as one might sit through an old Hitchcock film,
striated, jump-flicker, poor imaging
viewed each time in door-step de-gradations

remember how
in our childhood as all but siblings
we rang out over the rime, under arc-lights,
raced the marram grass to the sea

what now
but a favourite uncle's brass handles,
the lines in a scripted frown,
the fake grass presenting the open grave ?

and
in loose-leaf time
we will leave each other again
like abandoned receipts curling in an attic

so
straighten my smile
scrape the damp earth from your hug
and curb your impatience with minutiae

Nigel Humphreys

What Is Home?

Home is where we live.
Where we make love
conceive our children
wallow in communion.

Home is where we are
when we've nothing else.
Home is match-light that
catches fire or snuffs out.

Home is where hopes lie
dormant, breathing softly
in amniotic fluid
awaiting their stillbirth.

Home is where we hurt,
misplace our sense of worth.
Behind its closed walls
we parade our failings.

Home is where silence
can mean peace or anger.
Where our dreams crack
and we kill each other.

Home is where we dry,
slacken like aged skin.
Where we hope to die
alone or gripped by arms.

Michael Heery

Family Holiday

One summer, thirty years or more ago,
thunder-shards broke across
the wind battered hills of Wales.
Time hadn't yet caught up with itself:
strange unnatural phenomena were reported,
witnessed by the battle-surviving photographs.
The belief that everything would turn out alright
was etched into each choreographed pose.
Colours were less intense,
side by side, we smiled conspiratorially
and there again was the ubiquitous
red plastic bucket and spade
that followed us for a decade.

But we collapsed under the effort,
when we'd heard the shutter click and whir,
knowing our meagre familial joys
had been recorded for posterity.
For whom did we maintain the performance?
Those days slipped back and forth
on a knife's edge between
rural idyll and the raw hell
of being unnaturally enclosed
in unfamiliar space.
None of us knew how to behave:
to smile or snap,
how far to redefine our tolerance.
Uncertainty tensed our nerves
while proximity embarrassed us.

The little bedrooms were darkly oppressive,
rain water pounded the single window,
mud-caked shoes waited by the door,
bare cupboards mocked our empty stomachs
and a book left under a tree overnight
clotted into a pulp.
We strained towards breaking point
until the blessed relief
of car-loading for the mutual escape.
Home had never seemed so homelike.
Yet, looking back at those photos,
when we're spread across three counties,
I remember enjoying myself.

Amy Licence

Ancient Woodland

Like puppies the girls run on ahead
leaving the narrow path to the two of us.
My father is old, frail, anxious
doggedly following through the wood.
All around us the clamour of birds
from stooping bones of aged trees.
The lineage of lost coppices
seen splattered in lichen whorls.
When we rest he recalls a walk
with his own, long-dead father.

Heralds of this bedraggled wood
proclaiming moss, brambles, ivy
fallen tree trunks smothered in fungus
my father's shuffle, his unkempt hair
trumpet in one pure flourish
the singular beauty brought by time.
I hear the girls now, not far ahead
I sense behind, in single file
the company of our ancestors
that steady tread of the living and the dead.

Michael Heery

Lament: Britain BC

Come wind in the trees. Hear cries of the gulls. Beat stick upon
stone…

Bury my heart in the Neolithic
next to the burin spall piled high
leave me a spear that smells of the hunt
I'm seeking a stag's last breathing sigh.

Take me to Flag Fen's woven wattle
high over Creswell let me lie
hidden by grasses under a rain-shower
feeling the horses thundering by.

Arrow points chipped in afternoon sunlight
see how our children dance in the ring
building the barrow
bury the chieftain
listen; the women softly sing.

Bury my heart in the Neolithic
Mist of the Souls at hoar-frost time
lay me so gently; cast down the flowers
see the wild grasses glowing with rime.

Close by the Welland, down in the hollow
here set my bones in the fullness of days
nest of an eagle, seat of a hunter
pride of a leader, those were my ways.

Bury my heart in the Neolithic
what will I leave when memories fade?
trench the soil softly;
look oh so closely
see the dark stain that
my soul has made.

David Dennis

Where Waters Meet

There are places where waters meet,
Where streams flow down together.
Each from its own source arising,
And through different course running;
Through marsh and heather flowing,
By fields and overhanging shrubs;
From snowy summits and lonely lakes,
Twisting, turning, each its own way makes,
Gently in the warm sun; swiftly with the falling rain.

How simple is nature and yet so great
That when they meet, they in perfect unity
Flow down together to feed the thirsty sea.

John Appleyard

Horse Standing Motionless

Contentedness
is a horse standing motionless.

Nothing is required.
No need to graze or gallop.

Time and space are set at naught.
Not even a snort or a neigh.

There has been a demobilisation
of your horse senses.

Your personality is at one
with the windlessness of this summer day.

I think of a horseless carriage
with sugar lumps in its fuel tank.

You look sad, assailed by heavy thoughts,
as if some disappointment has paralysed you.

But you aren't.
You have no language for thoughts.

Neither are you in the kind of reverie
that fishermen know on the riverbank.

No. You lack even their ostensible aim.
Your mind is empty,

the state that Buddhist monks
aspire to in meditation.

This is the purest form of contentedness.
A horse standing motionless.

Duncan Fraser

A Visual Feast

Set dawn on a plate of morning light
sprinkled with night's dew.
Fill it with rising sun
and the chorus of wakening birds.
Let my eyes taste the arrival of day.

Slice me a diet of sunshine and rain.
Pierce thunderous skies
with forks of lightning.
Spoon up softening snow
and flavour it with a sparkle of frost.

Carry the seasons in a dish.
Let me sample freshness of Spring,
partake of Summer's succulence,
delight in Autumn's harvest,
and devour Winter's crispness.

Bring me sunset in a cup
steaming with the red of dusk.
Let me imbibe its fading colours
and swallow its darkening shadows
in the thirst of twilight.

Angela Bradley

The Wasp

Pale autumn sunshine in the late afternoon
warms a builder's barrow still on the drive,
filled with a load of aggregate, in which
a wasp clings to the rest of his short life.

His black and yellow stripes absorb the sun,
a droopy male half-stoned in a desert
of coarse sand and rough gravel, marooned
by seasonal tragedy, bearings lost, inert.

He harbours a morbid fascination for his harsh
surroundings, the use of his fragile wings gone,
delicate extracts of transparent film,
unable to lift him from a deep depression.

His thin legs start scrabbling manfully against
the odds, like fingers delving through rubble
for survivors. His bulbous eyes, observing
many surfaces, see nothing but trouble,

and no future, for even the shoot at the front
of the wheelbarrow is inclined to stop
his feeble efforts. Humanity, purely by chance,
has prevented him from rising to the top.

Too dozy to beat a half-hearted swat,
but with determination beyond his size, he tries
repeatedly to scale the heights, but to no avail,
and eventually, curled up like a foetus, he dies.

In the balance of sharp sand and gravel,
his slender wasted body surrenders to its fate,
catching the sunlight for one last moment,
and then lost forever among the aggregate.

Keith Shaw

Joni in Big Yellow Marigolds

If starlings were as rare as kingfishers,
wouldn't we flock to the kitchen window,
whisper, point and lurk behind the curtain -
our photographs would win awards.

Three starlings in the bird bath:
Baroque automata, bronze wings thrashing water,
flash translucent glazes - forest, damson, sloe -
set off by studded rows of smallest pearls;
in metallic tick-tock chorus
all raising beaks chipped sharp from yellow bone.

But there are only starlings in the garden,
beating up a chaffinch and scoffing the bluetits' seeds
and splashing all the water out of their bath.
So we fill up the kettle, wash the car,
load dishwashers, tumble dryers and easy planes,
await the day when starlings are as rare as kingfishers.

R D Gardner

Each Fall I Rise

It may be due to all those years of school
But as the crowds start to wind down the year
And as the heat starts to fade down to cool
The sound of rain is all I want to hear.
The trees put on a gown of red and gold
Then dance it off to be left stark and old.

All those back from the sun think me a fool
To want the cold breeze to nip at my ears.
A swirl of leaves will thrill me as a rule,
Both here and now and in thoughts of past years.
I know one year I will not beat the cold,
'Til then I'll let the chill winds make me bold.

Valentin Barrios-Ambroa

Reading the Diaries

You're dead since being there.
As good as. Nothing's real.
The present pounds you like a grudging tide.
You say you hate the place,
when driven there against your will
look at your feet. The mention makes you wild.

It reaches for you with sea tentacles
that stroke you restless in the night.
On hollow days you feel the throb
of foghorns where they don't belong

calling you traitor for turning
pages, flipping through the years.

But I was crazy then.
Like glaze on old stuff, chicken wire,
it got so far way, obscured;
the startling voice of someone else,
a favourite niece or young friend.
Far too cheerful and a little absurd.

I float in dark seams striving
to smooth the dog-eared mess,
but trying not to unfold it all too far.

Andria J Cooke

Falling in Love with Emma Peel

Before colour television,
which wasn't natural,
the make do and mend decades
were measured by coat hangers.
After ten years of good use
the suit from Moss Bros,
fabric for high days,
for charabanc and trolley days,
slid down the rail, second best,
and second went to the allotment,
patched and creosote stained.

When I began to know him,
to store him in my solid state,
he only ever wore gardening,
and on a Saturday afternoon
he drank medicinal brandies
thumping the arm rest, shouting
at Jackie Pallo and Mick McManus.
He was solid in monochrome,
immortal, locked in thrift, quiet,
unsinkable, but most importantly, mine,
and as a treat on Friday nights,
him in his chair and me on the rug,
we'd share Edam and Marmite on Ryvita
watching Emma Peel high kick
her way into our hearts.

Clive Gilson

Stray Cat

We were adopted by a feral cat
before you died, a big brash ginger tom,
a handsome pair of furry bollocks slung between his legs.

Against your protest, I said:
"They have to go!"
and hauled him off for surgery.

He has them still:
His balls are smaller, and inert,
but, to my surprise, intact.

Vasectomies for cats?
That seems to be the latest way of it.

It's tamed his wanderlust for sure,
his energies now firmly set on sovereignty
he biffs to kingdom come
all cats who dare to cross the line.

Expecting nothing, I caress his fur,
glad he is here
now you are not.

Stephen Firth

Play It Again Sam

Music is dangerous
for those with a past.

The moonlight kind
leads into wild alluring places,
behaves like innocuous wine,
wraps in desirable embraces,

brings face to face with mad near misses,
tastes of midnight toast, forbidden kisses,
slaps and shakes up, jerks out tears,
feels like heaven, rolls back years.

All music is sad music
for those who love
to listen to it.

Andria J Cooke

Days When Women Dance

I am the man
who holds up
the shield when the women come
out to dance.

First is expectation,
then excitement, then,
as always,
there will be one man
who will try to get past me,
and is taken.

The fourth day is saddest,
because the women go
and the man
is put to death.

But he didn't stop
the dancing,
and the women
will dance
again
next year.

r v jones

Landlines

Hearing without seeing
is like moving without being.

Your voice from nowhere
falls in pieces,
snakes, vibrates,
creates a fountain in my brain,
paints mindscapes
in iridescent skeins.

Each word curls out of you
a chrysalis that breaks its bonds
with the smallest of sounds,
a whispered kiss.

My replies resemble moths.
They flutter and pulsate
I go blank, become invisible,
while every pulse inflates.

Our sighs are fireflies
sent sparking through the miles
of midnight wires.

The merest breath balloons,
grows massive as the star-flecked sky.

Goodbye echoes goodbye.

Andria J Cooke

The Exchange of Chocolate for a Secret

At school,
when she was young,
she won a prize
for writing a story
about chocolate,
her reward,
a certificate,
six bars of chocolate,
cheers from her class,
she licked her lips
in anticipation.

On her way home,
a classmate stopped her,
I'll tell you a secret
if you give me one of those,
he whispered,
so she did,
the desire to know
was worth just one,
I love you,
he said,
and fled.

Back home,
high expectations,
proud parents,
five bars of chocolate,
but she never told them
about the missing bar,
the exchange
of chocolate
for a secret
had been as daring
as the kiss.

Gilly Jones

Pearl

Named for a gritty start:
abandoned in the street, aged two
diagnosed as mentally subnormal.
Foster care enclosed
her innocence in a shell.

Come twenty, institutionalised
but with a lustrous face
Pearl joined drama therapy.
Initially slow of speech
seeded with confidence
she opened like a sea-anemone.

One day she said to me
You're my only friend.
At my protest, *Only one in my life*
not mental, or paid to care.

Her group performed their piece
for parents, carers, students.
From grains of sand
they built a castle
harvesting first success.

Classes resumed, but Pearl was absent
her iridescence greatly missed.
I enquired of staff: we stared into
the muddy waters of abuse
pearls and swine came to mind.
The male carer moved on.
Pearl crept back into her shell.

Margaret Eddershaw

Peter Likes To Laugh

Peter likes fun.
He hoots like a train
laughs like a drain
a pun is too sly

for Peter. He is brimful
of chuckles, stuffed with guffaws
a barrelling bellyful
of hilarious applause.

He's a merry-go-round bellow
that eclipses the sun,
a roller-coasting holler
an explosion of fun

helter-skelters of laughter
spiral up from his toes
a headlong pell-mell
just waiting to blow

the roundabout echoes
ring in the air. You might say
he's a man who hasn't a care.
Peter is all the fun of the fair.

Marilyn Francis

Brief Sparkling Moments

Snowflake crystals fascinate me,
enchant with their unique shapes,
sparkle in the sunlight,
brilliant for such a short while
because although the sun
makes them stand out so bright
in their shining beauty,
it causes them to sadly melt,
dissolve and disappear
to water drops as wet as tears.

She beguiled me when I saw her,
she enchanted everyone
when she sang on that stage,
she was brilliant and beautiful,
all diamonds and sparkles,
she adored the limelight,
but when the applause stopped,
all the bright lights went out,
she dissolved into tears
and never performed again.

Gilly Jones

Empty Nest Syndrome

When the children left home
I started making nest-boxes,
little draught-proofed spaces
between sawn boards.

The fragrance of wood excited me:
cutting to size, drilling entrance-holes,
felting the small, sloping roofs.

Each box has a removable panel
for cleaning out at the end of the season,

which is the job I do this winter morning
now my fledglings have flown.

R J Hansford

Heave, Rewind

From sitting in the driving seat I grunt and heave
my body to a new position, swing out, just to leave
the car. I make a noise like lifting weights

And no, I am neither gross or fat, but inside some elastic
part of me has come undone, I think, and what was juice
and smooth and slick in me now grinds. In fact

there are some parts of me metallic, rearranged.
Unkind, maybe you could laugh, say I don't fire now
on every cylinder. Perhaps the blame

is thirty years of relative inaction
or harsher still, three decades of putrefaction, ha-ha
it's what they call getting old. But I need to say

my mind is faster, sleeker, now, craftier than then
when I could spring and dive and race and leap
from love to love and sleep to dreaming. I mean

faster, better than then. Now I am freer, much more
than then, when with glee and slobbering leer
I imagined various pudenda. I was young, but

after the snuffling, came the settling, then begetting
even if I felt like a spectator, waiting for the ads
and produced a wife and kids, moved on, seven years

produced another set, switched off, and then, back on again
didn't recognise the programme, felt it all lacked
depth or quality, something that the viewer brings

if only it was interactive, higher definition, the colours
sharper, maybe that would please, and now they say I can freeze
the living moment, pause, rewind, stop

to make a drink, answer the telephone, send an email,
and then continue. Oh sure, continue, but not go back
and change. Not a thing, just perspective.

r v jones

Chemotherapy

Dad! DAD!
from the other room
followed by
patterned slapping
of running feet.

Dad, guess what?
Excited tone
pitched high
and breathless.
Eyes at my face
like supernovas.

Look, Dad!
Chemotherapy.
It contains the word
mother.

Her burning eyes
proclaiming
comfort,
hope,
the magic of signs.

Michael Heery

Nil by Mouth

Sometimes you say
The first thing you see:
A football, some grass,
A feather, a tree.
Sometimes you just say
The first things that you see.

Sometimes all you
Seem to do is talk,
And miss the very thing
You'd hoped to see.
Sometimes you just
Talk, and talk, and talk.

Sometimes you sit here,
In the same room as me,
And I wonder what you're thinking,
And I wonder what you see.
I wonder if you tell it to the ocean,
Because you never tell me.

Valentin Barrios-Ambroa

A Special Way of Being Afraid

Last night I dreamt
I went to Basingstoke again, to mow
something to do with grass but
the mower stalled, twice, and kneeling
I found the blades choked,
with lily-pads and sea
anemones,
anemones!

But then I thought, running
on empty, the mower is not
clogged, it needs sustenance
petrol, two-stroke, oil
to calm the seas

My age, fallen, floats away
like a soap sud: Where's the looney
bin? It's possibly plastic, must be
here somewhere.

Boys dream of native girls and breadfruit
politicians Chappaquiddick
moguls a place to suck a buck
while I have accidentally started
an avalanche
while putting out fire

I am no longer sure If I am
animal, vegetable or mineral?

This is a special way of being afraid.

r v jones

Where Does Truth Come From?

Unfurled from dark cypress leaves
scented of the East; in clean acidity
of lime and lemon, the scurvy battlers;
from cool Norway's fjords and mute
blood-darkness of the old world;
from the drag of a hunter's catch;
in caves and flicker-lit halls;
in sagas sung to the rub of
skin on skin at midnight.

Knowing the time, decades passed
into static sepia, of a child
carefully dressed to play upon
a lawn tended by gardeners'
hands, of lupin and foxglove,
cloudy baths before bedtime
where limbs surface like bergs,
dreaming of adulthood and
the next shift in understanding.

From the imminent approach;
the arrival of train, or guest for
a night, from lips of lovers
soon to part, from the broken promise,
the unused wedding dress,
the static line of helpless traffic
stuck on the arterial crepuscular
and the silence of the moment
when we must depart.

Amy Licence

vermicelli

worms
nest in
dreams,
as she writes
they react to
the lightning
of image,
traffic of
thought,
their bodies
articulate
in hoop
segments,
they have
neither eyes
nor ears and
never sleep,
lacing within
the cortex they
break down
notions into
pulses for
encrypting
and dissemination,
each receptor ingests
a concept or image
and begins its journey
along the neural pathway
by way of the ulna to the
fingers' extremity; they wire
down the quill's shaft and
pipe through the calumus
onto her scented notepaper
morphing delicately
into coded sculptures,
the writing completed
her maid hosts them
to her lady's lover, he
violates the seal careless
of contagion and her worms
piggy-back light into his eyes
wriggle up the optic nerve
and work on his brain
converting his composted
independence into loam

Nigel Humphreys

65

The Komodo dragon

The Komodo dragon is a lugubrious lump
That prefers to spend its day contemplating

Bookcases

Or the gold-trims surrounding dubious titles
Ornately incised, decorating the spines
Of various Leather book-bindings

Nodding interest in suitable style: perpetually erudite
Might briefly open one eye and rarely smiles
At new-fangled Scientific-findings

Before chewing its gums, as it fritters its time
It basks in the sun dribbling bloody saliva
Alchemically comparable to foaming liquid fire
Hence earning its name, its claim to fame
Its nasty bite of fluid-flame
That leaves its prey septicaemically dying

Which is why the Komodo dragon prefers not to examine
Or ascertain how dinner dies;
Agonizingly slow with a pain which has little in common
To spending a day looking glum: contemplating

Book-cases

Karl Ghattas

Poetry Is...

Poetry is the ghost of memory,
a memory of ghosts. It is a dream
forgotten as we wake: an infant's scream
of joy or fear, the moaning of the sea.
It is the light that strikes a flooded fen,
the lisp of streams over a gravelled bed.
It is the empty yearnings of the dead,
the anvil's fading spark, the rainbow's end.
It is the wail of wind through belfry towers,
the cry of winter geese from snow-dark skies;
the hum of bees, the whirr of damselflies,
the symphonies of songbirds after showers.

Poetry is the thoughts that lovers send
across dark continents to the world's end.

Phil Powley

Fertility

I am tired of poems
their long gestation and difficult births;
too often they are stillborn.

I must take precautions
against the womb-wrenching pain
of flesh become word.

I still produce one every year
despite the use of douche and pessary.
Who could thwart immaculate conception?

R J Hansford

67

Secret Windings

Asleep,
eyelids closed
soft as soot-fall
on secret White Rabbit dreams,
I follow a timeless tick-tock spiral.
Look. No hands.
Watch me fall.
Watch me fly
headlong into darkness

on a never-ending staircase
the *Nu Descendant* clicks into
clockwork shards of motion
in a perpetual state of becoming
a cobra slowly uncoils
in a charmed
circle of
sound
reality is unwinding
unravelling
it dissolves
turning
in a sickening vortex
down, down
to the Davy Jones
deeps
of
the
night.

Marilyn Francis

Editor's Note

The poets featured in this book include the winner of the WordArt 2007 poetry competition, Phil Powley, and a selection from the WordArt shortlists: Angela Bradley, Andria J Cooke, Gilly Jones, Valentin Barrios-Ambroa and Alison Craig. The winner of the Earlyworks Press Open poetry competition, Margaret Eddershaw, opens this collection. Her work is accompanied by the top twenty poems and a selection from the Earlyworks Press Writers and Reviewers Club.

If you enjoyed **Shoogle Tide**, we'd like to recommend:

Routemasters & Mushrooms

a selection from the first Earlyworks Press Competition. Critics have said:

Earlyworks Press is off to a good start with their first anthology – an intriguing title, and some excellent and varied poems from such well-known names as Roger Elkin.
Phil Fox for instance, serves up a sensuous dish About Tarts whilst Duncan Fraser's speciality is the wry humour of High Rising Terminal. More poignant notes are struck by Sally Richards in Institutional, Angela Rigby, describing Last Rites and Jane Moreton's evocative Coach Journey: Half-Light.

– Carole Baldock, Editor of Orbis.

An interesting mix of very good poetry. The Routemaster might be decommissioned, but it's proven an unexpected source of inspiration for just one poem in a compilation that ranges from the reassuringly familiar to the cosmic in scope. Not a single bland, run-of-the-mill poem in the mix.

– DJ Tyrer, Atlantean Publishing

Routemasters & Mushrooms published by Earlyworks Press
ISBN 978-09553429-0-5   **£5.50** + £1 p & p to UK addresses

In a lighter mood, you could try:

Porkies – Pigtales of the Unexpected

Sweet and sour bites of life from the Earlyworks Press writers. It's enough to drive a prawn crackers! Here are a few samples:

by David R Morgan...

Limerick

There was a young teacher from Staines
Who simply hated the use of canes:
He had other controls
For deviant souls,
Such as plugging them into the mains.

Compute This

It was the night before Christmas, when all through the house
Not a creature was stirring except father's mouse.
The computer was humming; the icons were hopping,
As father did last-minute Internet shopping.

The stockngs were hung by the modem with care
In the hope that St Nicholas would bring new software.
The chldren were nestled all snug in their beds,
While visions of computer games danced in their heads.

The letters to Santa had been sent out by mom,
To santaclaus@toyshop.northpole.com
Which has now been re-routed to the United States
Because Santa's workshop has been bought by Bill Gates.

by Kay Green...

Vicarious Daffodils

My sister wandered like a lonely cloud
With corsets, cumb'ring veils and heels
When all at once she had a crowd
Of lucid, tingling new ideas.
Sister dearest, write them down for me,
Alchemy incarnate! - A poet, we!

by Terry Sorby...

Grunts

Oink - Oink - Oink -
he glanced down the road
looking for a pig
and was run over
by a veteran car.

   * * *

He ate like a hog
pigging his face.
I got boared
and left the swine
to sow my oats with Bill

   * * *

There was an old lady who swallowed a sow.
I don't know how
she swallowed a sow
it could have been her big gob.

   * * *

This little piggy went to market
This little piggy stayed at home
This little piggy had bread and jam
This little piggy had none
And this little piggy read up on shopaholics,
agoraphobia, obesity and farming subsidies.

Lots more gigglesome poems, plus stories with a twist by Terry
Sorby, C R Krishnan, Victoria Seymour, Nigel Humphreys, Kay
Green and Sally Richards and illustrations by Kath Keep, Katy J
Jones, Wendy Lane and Nikola Temkov

Porkies – Pigtales of the Unexpected pub Earlyworks Press
ISBN 978-09553429-1-2   **£6.50** + £1 p & p to UK addresses

Our lists include more poetry books, literary and genre fiction and we also promote a variety of fiction and non-fiction books by independent writers. All Earlyworks Press books are available direct from our website at www.earlyworkspress.co.uk or can be ordered from independent bookshops. (You can order them from Amazon or from big chain bookstores too but we are independents and we believe everyone benefits more if the profits go to small companies and creative communities.)

If you are a writer and would like to submit work for the next book, go to the competitions page at www.earlyworkspress.co.uk for details, or write to Kay Green, The Creative Media Centre, 45 Robertson Street, Hastings Sussex TN34 1HL.

If you would like to join in our online workshops, use our services to writers or have space on our website to promote your own writing or artwork, please visit the Club and Stepping Stones pages at…

www.earlyworkspress.co.uk

And finally …

our sincere thanks and good wishes to all in the Earlyworks Press online club who gave help and encouragement along the way, and to the East Sussex County Library and Information Services, who contributed to the printing costs for this book.

Kay Green, June 2007